A Stab in th

Bengt O Björklund

ISBN-13: 978-1985616479

ISBN-10: 1985616475

ALIEN BUDDHA PRESS 2018

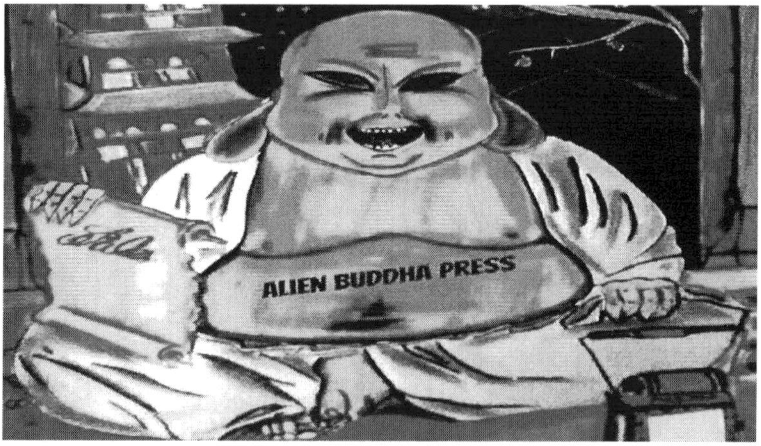
ALIEN BUDDHA PRESS

Cold Grass................. 5

Saturated...................12

Whirling.....................20

Old Man.....................26

Cloaked Severity........32

Elevators...................38

Torched.....................40

Deeds Cringe..............45

Startled......................46

Dark Deeds.................50

Definitions..................54

Scrawny.....................59

Tools of Weird Lore....62

No Hidden Agenda..... 67

Old Sorcerer................72

First Soil.....................74

Selected.....................78

1

Cold grass sways their bold necks,
indifferent to the season's grim tale,
too short to be told more than once
this long, unsteady night.

The sounding drums of war.
Bleeding, bleeding…
The reckoning of days.
The hollow eye.

A bird above the barren froth
sings of grass in crystal silence,
calling no more.
Families and trees, all gone.

Fathers long before us
waited for their turn to fill the gap.
The sun in a sea of salt.

Seep through weeping autumn
with gales and gusts,
with weird tools of dark mystery.

Old man hears bells of sunken ships
calling in the weeping mist called memory
if there only was a book of codes.

Thrusts of pain spear Old man's hope
of ever joining joy's magical
master switch
with its ascendance
into a clear cerulean forever.

"Speak you bloody tongue
of all that matters;
speak of all things unsaid,
unheard of amongst beasts,
hovering in halls
yet unmeasured by eyes."

Leaves of old age fold,
as they should and must;
the soaked soil
knows the downward direction,
the falling spells its name.

This he knows,
that in between this
and what really goes on
there are eyes
dying to get closer.

Driven by the heavy toll
chimney sweeps might allow,
Old man forges day's insanity
into the one true sword
cold nights insist upon.

Never promised by tomorrow,
his scarecrow fingers beckon.
Mortally wounded
he falls short at midnight.

Once milky skin
embraced his dreams
with warm anxiety,
gulls hung above the sea.

Now he is bruised remains,
eyes falling, leaves.
Earth's dark, exhausted bowl
carries his tenderness.

Dreams fill his days,
sleep erases all hope;
a sullen mound, even more so.
The wind crawls
like a quiet sarcoma patient

over grassy knolls in desperation,
hollering at midnight
with an intent beyond the stars:

"Leave me not to time's device,
Nor to the sound of seashells
breaking on wet slabs;
let gentle perish be my hollow mass,
all my broken feet will ever know."

Measuring all dark hills
I, a cerulean horizon, commences.
Old man purges the passing
with one simple word
and another one leaping
like wind's revision from trees
that gives him a different sea.

Memories of an old town
move through the wet woods
of a bare November gaze.

Ice-stars roll across sheep hills,
dare the thought to be I see,
a memory hidden in dark waves
of lost childhood summers.

Clean, white water
once ran transparent
under these my I stones;
feathery ferns called
for a viridian indulgence;
birds hid in green, soporific shadows.
Bright chlorophyll
rolled like dark thunder.

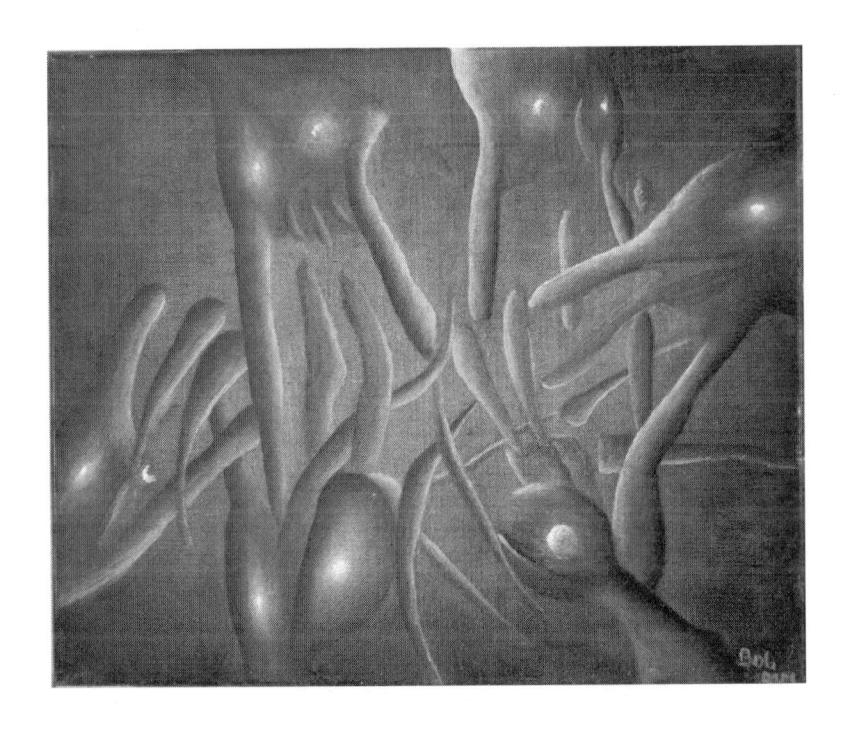

"All Hands Aboard, 2001"

2

Saturated in a circular perfection,
not yet pale in a flawless winter sky,
the gritty moon wages war
for yet another way to inherit.
Sparrows fold their day in quiet merit,
there are tales of feathery fames.

Once the grass was tall and free,
slow nights carried windy messages
across a perfectly curved sky.
Now the grass is hurriedly trimmed short
for a final, concave hour
with a mercury motion, down.

Bold, defying cries of departing birds
roll across still roadside tombs.
Old man finds no plea.
Never again shall his prayers
fall in love so easily
with crude saxophones on the radio.

Regal rises above hushed trees,
bare with a dark, stiff tongued itching;
the night is a silent belonging.
He has known that coming
long before these words.

Wild wings of a floating elegance
ride dark water's slow goodbye;
songs of the grave jelly fish
break the long time coming.
Abandoned ferries ruptures,
expecting snow's illumination.

The old man waits for darkness
in leaps and recoils,
unprepared for the sound
bass players can make;
there are stiff remembrance reeds
in a lost sea of horns.

The eye, heavy with night,
colors all that might be;
the I rises, yet falls heavily
where many an I walks,
continuing the warped distance
from here to another now.

Tall night falls with dervish snow.
Green grass groomed in white,
in an icy tell tale spell grandeur,

beckons to sparrows in bare bushes,
cringing in an I dark suspension.

When darkness finally tolls
in rooms of bad surgery
he discovers another see saw syllable,
his hands are signs in a timeless tale.
Slow shadows are lost to opportunity;
crossroads transmute, wither and leave.

There are winds that can mold hearts of snow;
white birches that can bow, twig strung,
to sky's dark encounter with no more
yesterday.
Suburbia, evening's dark companion,
abandons misery and runs for lost causes.
The voices of dead children

freeze in formalin over bedsides
where visions call
for pale pastoral stories to continue
with wintry fantasies and laughter.

A breath of irrevocability
cloaks the dying of the day;
images of ancient ships
sail into a long goodbye sun.
There are no more pages.

Old man in the night city
howls into a heedless night.
There is an old shortage of cedar.

Dog tired man bones
slowly rot into mire mass,
in hollow perpetuation.
Smug charlatans hide

their dark deeds of pain
behind stiff-starched cloths
demanding silly ceremonies.

There are men dancing in oil
at the border of conflict,
residing in the erratic hour
of fear and dark terror,
just to make sure.

"Origin, 1999"

3

Whirling within limited existence, aroused,
crawling across weathered city centers,
Old man foresees all he is not
and dares the rest to find its own peace
with what is no longer possible.

Itchy with incorrigible ways
he cringes at the touch of the one word,
pointing at him. He is lost.
His defiant smile breaks the moon,
his intentions are hung like pale stars
on long lines of considerations.

The sky is a sea-fading fish bone,
a struggle amongst wiry clouds
where winds interpret, or change
the fate of lost men calling
with their pockets full of saved images,
grinning over dark, watery graves.

Tangled in a warm hide,
breathing softly beneath contortions,
Old man dares not to fall
into night's justified wrath,
he dares not invoke origin
where darkness sieges all ending days.
Overlapping moments of tolling now
fall unexpectedly into his lap.

Old man's love is a like merry icon,
a slow dissolve into soft cries
prying into the delving;

a muted call, fading into dawn;
there is no other.

His story is a bony tail,
a symphonic patriot at play.
He disbands and displays grey glory.
It is the ticking time he molds,
time that still will not play
with crude clay.

Who will dare dark incitement,
daily flights no hidden man can heed?
Old man feeds no flare, no fight,
nor what his bare needs can prey upon
in nights that bleed for no more.

Thus he calls the pending year
by all fear night concludes in cries;
abandoned kites run amongst small stars,
soar in their wondrous wake.

This is nothing more than a glimpse,
a voyage of no consequence,
winding its way from here
to a potential said so
and all the way back again.

Drab stories of delusion fall short at dusk.
Frenzied voices from subzero continents
slide down dark moon's pale matter,
looking for a chance
to meet what will not come.

Colliding carelessly with
salty wood-words of winter,
black crows, with feathery bets,
Old man beats the collectors
to the meltdown.

Food is the final curtain call.
Old predator blinds
hang broken and deadly vicious
in a way that time neglects
in chains and with no peace.

Oxygen is more
than just a lethal breath.
Tuition so much more
than just coercion.

4

Old man war and solitude
finds himself armed and ready
with a righteous howl
and brittle bones to go.

The power of money
makes for a long term claim
of all that tags along.
Hypochondriac men
claim dominance by default.

Glossy shadows of power
feed on pain's given illusion,
focuses on self-imported
aspects of visibility.

Daring is a glorious move
with no need for blood taken
or a religious fervor
to defend the order of dark deeds.

Old man walking
sees flaws at the fundament,
a keep safe illusion,
a mind's complication.

A tumbling today, no direction.
A melting-point leaping
as he, as it were, hoped to canalize
the potential of a lame future
into pools of consideration.

Old man is wild intention
bleeding weary night goodbye,
he is too bold to be daft or even stale,
too rapt to pale or fold.

He is shift change from cruel tears
into one more Good night.

The sound of sirens echoes
with fractal consideration
in halls where danger falls short
at mercury midnight's
bright titan call for moderation.

Never before did a whispered moon
rip at the core of mortal serendipity
with such a definite intent,
never before had it occurred to him
that the haste of days is hereditary.

The waning moon has spent
all its expensive emission
on cellular mass-calls for dawn.
Bright nimbus of winter distortion
warps the distance into a frosty glass
where drops softly freeze
into another oblivion.

At the dull hour of leaving,
when light of other days
imbues all he can see,
when being breaks into longing
and matter makes a million goodbyes,
each a sweet bead on a lost rosary,
it is then defeat is bearable.

Parting is a billion suns
bursting into flames
in a single piece of dry wood;
conceding is to swell in that light

with each breath of hot burning air.
Cause has no other origin.

Old man turns in his sleep
just before next day
beckons with a new horizon.

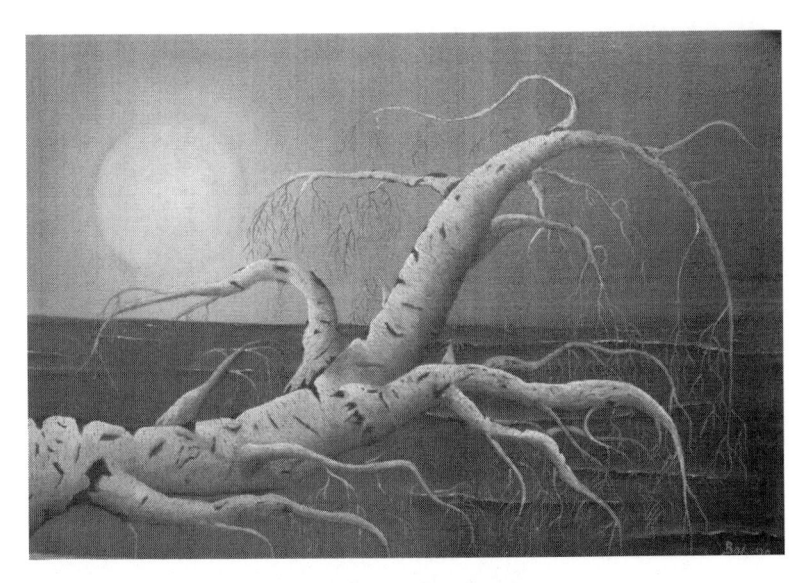

"Dragon Birch, 1998"

5

Old man downs cloaked severity
at daybreak's first call
on his way to close his heart and tale
on a cold and flawless winter day.

Turning all bold forever's
into rolling fire
beneath a cold private sky
he cries for the children,
burning in books lost.

Bushes etched in winter nudity,
exudes bright flittering clouds
of a warm, feathery life.

Tears of irrevocability
ices the slow sea
where mighty mackerels hum.

He must forego all masters of oblivion
on his way to the sea.
A billion tears
have not flowed in vain.

Old man's final call will soon
roll fatal life's condition
and nothing but broken tail lights
will guide the concluding of the day.

Slandering seas will die,
– before breakfast –
in a temporal disgust, lust
as a slow burning;
jellyfish moves in contempt.

It is persistence
that holds him fretting
and falling.
The falling could have kept him
from staring at the end.

"Good night weary wisdom's fading.
Tonight no one can play elusive
with the smile of pale stars.
Shadows will not play."

Death has no further say
when it falls into broken night;
haunting rites and intangible ends
give wind to voices lost in blame,
lament and salt.

Time is cruel at midnight's falling.
Water puts shanty towns to sleep
above shimmering waves
and moon's skeletons dancing.

Theft is located somewhere
between the third and fourth vertebra,
signaling a lost tail.
Prostitution goes for the money
while translucent skin
tells another tale.

Codes of conduct define what he is
as he materializes in what he can see.
It is time to sleep.

"Only So Far, 2003"

6

Elevators rising far beyond

the wanted floor

turn into blue subways

with female drivers

shifting into new tracks

every time you look.

The phone rings.

You are in a tunnel.

Cellophane thoughts

of a certain cerulean sentiment

unfold a hollow multiplicity.

Old man is barely here.

Who then to challenge his appearance?

Night after night he scratches at origin,

dares specters to dance with him.

Night after night his proverbial spirit

longs for love's flickering sensation
a brief fleeting moment.

Soaring through the entire all of it
he embraces the irrevocable.
Speed is a lethal companion.

All possessions will transform
into bedrock, blood,
into bones and dreadful integrity,
the hesitancy of pale dust.

The city moves cadres of dead eloquence
down abandoned streets
where catafalques of lost innocence
roll like nothing more.

7

Torched by fire of oblivion
Old man longs for water
in the late rush hour cry,
for opium and hindsight,
for an ultimate here.

Memory is a fading legacy
balancing on salty sea words
with gravity imploding in images.
Only condition may redirect
what others say.

"Long live extreme and august anger
uniting roaming packs
that crave mass destruction
with words of blind dead want
and swords that flash
in no eloquent fashion."

Hot gain is far more exciting
than the anguish of poverty.
A dark heart speaks loud.
On the unpaved streets
the infamous scrounge
for a piece of blue sky.

"Long live the voices
that pray for blood,
unforgiving instigators
of fear and cold obliteration."

Winter began with a blue gentleness,
dancing in soft circles of integrity;
the peripheral encouraged mild control
as a matter of being in charge.

All that he is and all that he does
leaps at the touch of sudden snow.
Morning is merely the name
of a new white intention.

Glowing in an insidiously timed sea,
suspended like surprised herons,
turning curved, beady beaks
toward a concluding surf,
Old man dives into the here and now
for a glimpse of harnessed light.

Calamities toll like metal shadows
in the eye of the witness.
Weight fills his recollection
with even more regret.

"Cry you hollow man;
the wind is still in your shoes.
No one will follow you;
the echo of circular water
is only sand in your timed tumbler."

Daring dark day's profundity
Old man slows down,
facing inevitability.
The day's daring process
collides with intention to express;
the dance subsides;
what must be said is lost.

For a moment he is caught
in the middle of history
with the best of all intention.
The distance between what has been
and what will come
carries his first name.

Webs within circles of distraction
often hold his attention
as day follows moon
on its way to forgetfulness.
The electric night,
baleful with harsh light,
is a vigilant eye.

A dog carries his smile,
he is dark day with intentions.
He is the light in the hall
when the fuse is lit.
Never looking back
he finds the wind irresistible.

8

Deeds cringe at dark wood's end,
slither and die over leafy lips.
He hesitates,
although this particular crossing
is of no value.
Nevertheless, there are phantoms
attacking his conscious effort.

It is here he might meet what is
without slow cloaks of misrepresentation,
here, where telltale custom officers
cast anesthetized spells in shadows.

Never before has he been so fraught
with a rendezvous of this kind,
binding fractured perception
into one single moment.
There is no other touch.

Scavenging scholars of grey intent
bleed across pillared temples of greed,
over crossbows and sugared lust,
dusty images of what will never be,
purple words all in disarray.

Elements of understanding
has to do with keys and clouds,
with a state of origin. Birthed mortals
need to breathe into the wild.

Tall night bear neither snow nor rain,
someone plays the piano.
Voices float like winter clouds
over possible objection.

"I do believe in the sound of words,
the spoken, the impossible,
the mad glimpses of belonging,
the electric flashes
between my bedroom poles,

the taut viridian wood
outside my window;
the moon is shifting."

The wind, the air he moves,
intentions that move him,
 — highways and wasteland —
cannot be collected in jars.

Slow is his purpose,
folding old maps all day.
Steeped like flooded beach,
he is intense, he leaps in bold jumps
over old findings.

Old man lost on the stage
finds night to his liking.
There is no other.

9

Startled by trivial words silently soaring
over snow's dark, fine cover,
Old man finds himself in disarray.

A host of long lost images plunges
through an early windy presence
demanding to be named and dear.

The sea rocks the day
into echoes that fly the light,
endlessly rolling a dark below.

He stands by the water,
horizon walks the distance
into a gulls sudden cry.

A Sunday morning bell;
eyes raced are still.
Glorious peace that eats the heart!

With all that and no regret
there's nothing more to covet.

For a moment he dangles;
a bait for the ambitious
and the totally ignorant.

No sweet aroma starfish
surfs dark water's curve.
Death has no say here,
fooled by a different charm.

The silvery cod tolls for all men,
limber squids fall for you,
grey clouds of shrimps,
colonies of wet clams
– weepy secrets
anchored to the foolish eddy –
fall into yesterday's said so.

10

Dark deeds wring their sweaty hands
where another man would just say:
"It costs to harbor volatile spirits
under capricious skin! Flee!"
Like a smoldering fire at midnight
cold December crumbles.

Night abducts his lost frenzy,
the seen puts mist into his sleep.

The math of the coroner's result
beds with the very best of our age,
cheered on by the lazy,
by the eyes of the confused in sleep.

Tonight all content is external.
The speed of the thermometer
is certainly of no avail to him
who no longer is alive,
there's no longer a physic content.

Winter breaks with chilly seals,
with lights from singular fires.
The touch, soft and discrete,
speaks of another old man in a cave.

A ray of hope cringes,
eats dark light and halts
before winter goes astray.

Drab sarcophagi of night
slide into flake white openings;
a dark eye, lost,
feeds on diatribes. There is no solace.

Who calls for more when it is dark?
Shadows of guilt flicker in rooms
where no house wolf ever reigned.
The air smells of more snow.

"Another Trinity, 1974"

11

Definitions of a see-through
whirl-like tainted rainbow
spanning dark cities
fill the early hour rising.

Indigested ceremonies of division
plunge without scope into lethargy,
the world is a setback,
talking nonsense by the window.

The conclusion of flickering loss
winds a ticking heart
minutes before clear sky
cracks up with ink of old.

The end of an imperfect day sinks
below what is left
of aspiration and hope,
loss is dragged down dull streets.

Brave intentions fold in sleep,
dark dreams approach at midnight.
What is gained will pass like mist,
evaporating figures of no logic.

Swirl you origin of unending watery curves,
you cause of bright flickering reflections
over bastions of no more faith
than in a ragged coastline struggle,
waves fettered at midair falling
merge in a lucid goodbye.

Singed "what ifs" curl and die
in faces slow with inevitability.
Weakness is a common name
when liquid is cheap
and illegal opaque essences
hide inside blue tonsils.

The ice van broke down at dawn,
forfeiting all motherly intent.
Planetary dreams surface
in a careful monetary surveillance.
Who sees the doorway?
Who baits continuance with precision?

Indecent spreads of desire
drift like smoke over old wisdom.
Genetic belongings are more
than a physical drive to run
for uncharted marshes
where songs burst into tears.

Slow back burning trains,
rail-sounding Indian tablas;
Old man bets his long lost tale
on the one night.

Cautious beneath a mask
of social charm
he talks freely by the bar.

"Daring the limited to move
is about all
one breath can muster
at a temporary wait station."

Threads of a new comprehension
pull at every day's withering say;
the silent agreement that comes
point carefree fingers.

No blame on him, though he stands to lose.
He is grief and sorrow.
He is not tomorrow.

Night might not find him another lover
silently turning different intentions

into different inevitabilities.

He might not survive,

though fidelity flies with the best.

12

Teenage girls, scrawny
like unfed geese in the spring,
float through harbor attention
on their way to blue ocean's loss
with only a smile to support them.

White froth fills the gate,
terms are not yet drawn.
What dark there is
murmurs in anticipation.

A thrust breaks the oily mirror,
A red buoy shines in silver light.
Not yet immortal
is all these girls can ask for.

Cranes in the old man's view
roll in a continuous aftermath.

Offspring flutters in chemic confusion,
lost seraphs and historic delusions,
all unfurl separate uncertainties
in nights with nothing more to say.

"Must the theory we all name days
be caught in midsentence
before what is can be implied?"

A leaded invoice fell by the gate,
there will be no more lethal fiascos
at the end of this sultry night.
Ships are moored.

There is more to the one hand
holding on to waves.
There is no reason why
A lost orphan cannot hoist a flag.

..

The girls still move like one
between tackle and bait.
There will be a final good night.

13

Tools of weird lore lend themselves easily
to the lost cures of ancient traditions,
playing in waves of blue dreams
where saxophones of old walk in line,
murmuring nonsense at midnight,
pointing at mislaid directions,
baffled by the mages of fake infinity.

Word substance flock at the foothills
with rolling water's entry shine
in pools of wet longing.
But he is lost.

Dark aspirations ignite the hills
where old poet in context
give birth and breathe.
The water hymen is broken.
It tolls in a different tale.

Lost in waves of slow extinction,
shaped by the agony of old mothers,
Old man cares not for the gloom
that fills everyone's periphery,
pointing away from the shore.

He walks not in today's peace,
nor beneath the wicker basket sun
of yesterday gone,
rolling across feathery fields,
hen-shaped and slowly dying away
before eyes can say goodbye.

It is a Mother of pearl morning,
– burning on the inside of a turtle shell,
smelling of wet decay and salt –
He mounts the sea with pain,
a serpent grinds his sand
and lights his wet weed,
stray birds shrieks in unison.

Day after driven day
Old man wrings a futile fire
lost middle men may scorn
in collect calls with consideration.

Midnight moon passes,
perpetuated by the ticking
of the old retreating heart.

All is contained in a manmade morning
where he stands by the window,
trading nebulous night for bright grief.

Teased by dark end's telltale perusal
he falls windward into wet grass calling.
The viridian is a dark horse.

The bellowing roar of water watched
breaks the distant seaweed summer

where vacant shells and dead fish are discarded.

Never before did a promise of continuance
roll morning into steeples and more cider,
with only a seahorse to plead with.

Old man is lost in views:
There never was anything else.
He is close to the going.
It is winter.

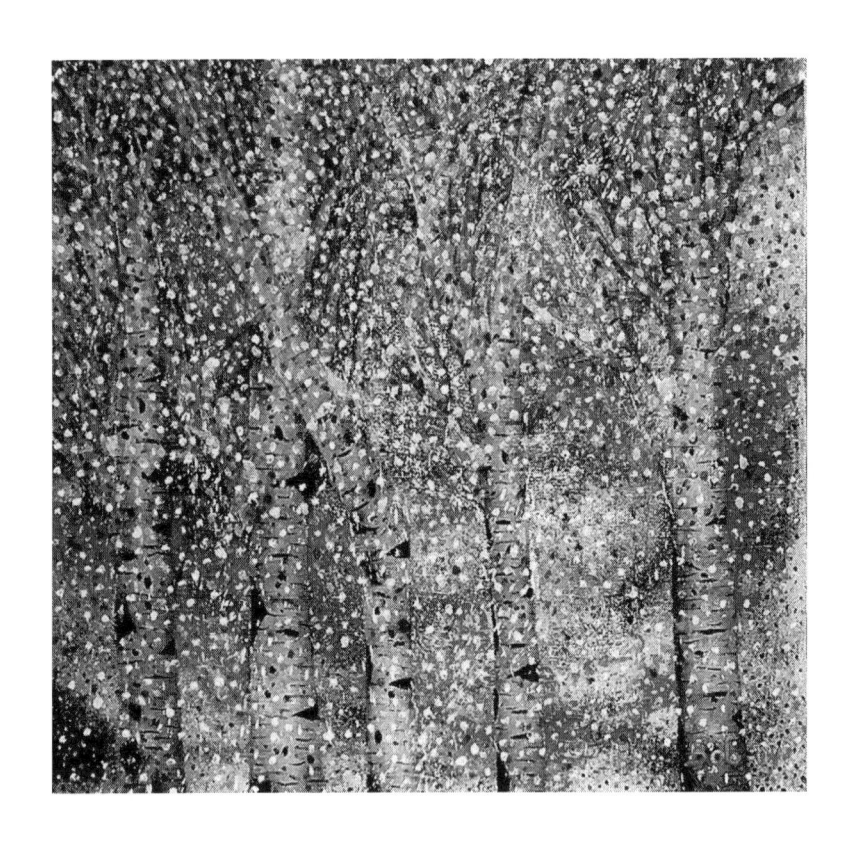

"Birches in the Snow, 2004"

14

There is no hidden agenda
Old man can rely on,
no cheerful day, no tapdancing
to fireflies and girls
on their way to the meat market.
Streets of silver
point to the fracture.

Bones that melted for Paganini
reinvents the way he falls,
a soft surrender flowing
beneath a cold sun humming.
He carries tall trees with him
and the dying of fish
falling in the grass.

Pale bones and summers gone
talk to the descending sea
where once wooden flutes
echoed out of sore groins
in silent whispers.

Fierce is the fire that feeds
on fake sainthood and salt,
on naked arms in cloth.
Watermills move to gullibility
and stiff collars at high noon.

Sureties are pale words on waves
rolling wet sand into bed.
A cat's smile folds fading silence
into dark water dreams.

Wild to the obnoxious bone
Old man tells his tale to the crowd
with no hope of a here
after the eleven sharp bell.

Stretched, corrupted and lost
in the brevity of life's commotion
Old man ploughs the earth
in his own slow fashion,
grieving for days to name.

Going down with thunder,
leaving the fat fabric of clouds
in the thick wake of yesterday,
– there is so much umbra –
he separates daybreak from wild water.

He will not die in dread or fear,
nor tolerate the coming of mean storms.
All is salt, vinegar and tears,
all is shape, longing,
seaweed standing tall.

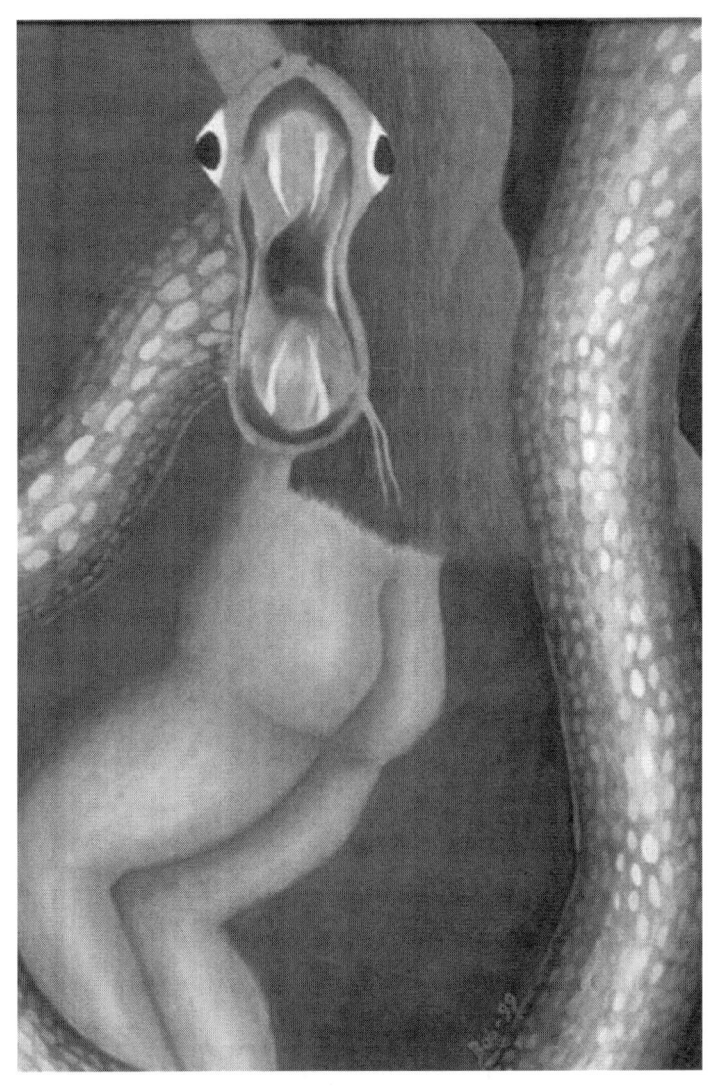

"Eve and the Snake, 1999"

15

The old sorcerer
summons his birds at dawn,
bedpans roll in the palm
of his other hand.
He wants more luminous rain,
more potent grass.

The second death came that dawn,
gulls and terns called into the light
just before bright rain and a soft wind
left night to prowl elsewhere.

Early birches, charged and soaked
by the edge of more rain,
told a different story,
unfurling green flags in a distant war
where mongrels and squatters
roll in accusation.

Distant bankers are squeezed
for more money
far into the burning dessert
where a parched scorpion
click beneath a harsh crescent.

Migratory whispers
around lakes, in trees and high above,
herald thunder with beady eyes.

The shaman's shoes are gone
with a slow brooding light.
The passing of dreams
roll over wet grass and pillows.

There is a no more in all
the wonderfully cloaked
floating by his side.

16

"I am the first soil,
the breeding ground
where all conscious efforts
toll in open windows."

Wine flows on red walls,
sirens interfere
with dead streets walking;
thugs feast on low visibility.

Money makes bombs
that make children burn.
Fingers itching with power
run like hysterical fires
through insolent hair.

Captured giants
roll down
scorched hills,

break into villages
with no cheers.

Old man dreams of a free world
where there is no need
for fat children to eat,
for free fall teenagers in suicide mode,
the daredevils old scribes forgot
while copying myths before the fall.

There is a booming darkness
rising over Gilgamesh mountain,
long before he was renamed
into Moses.

There are rivers of tears
running through the valleys
where cedar and cannabis
once spiced the air,
where the olive was a deity
long before the flood.

A poor shepherd boy strapped
belted death to his day.
His much loved goat turned missile
for the sake of a different tale
where Ur no longer echoes.

Shamash! Ki! Inanna!
Sumerian ghosts
still sing in the shadows
where villages still bleed
in Old man's sleep.

"I, 2002"

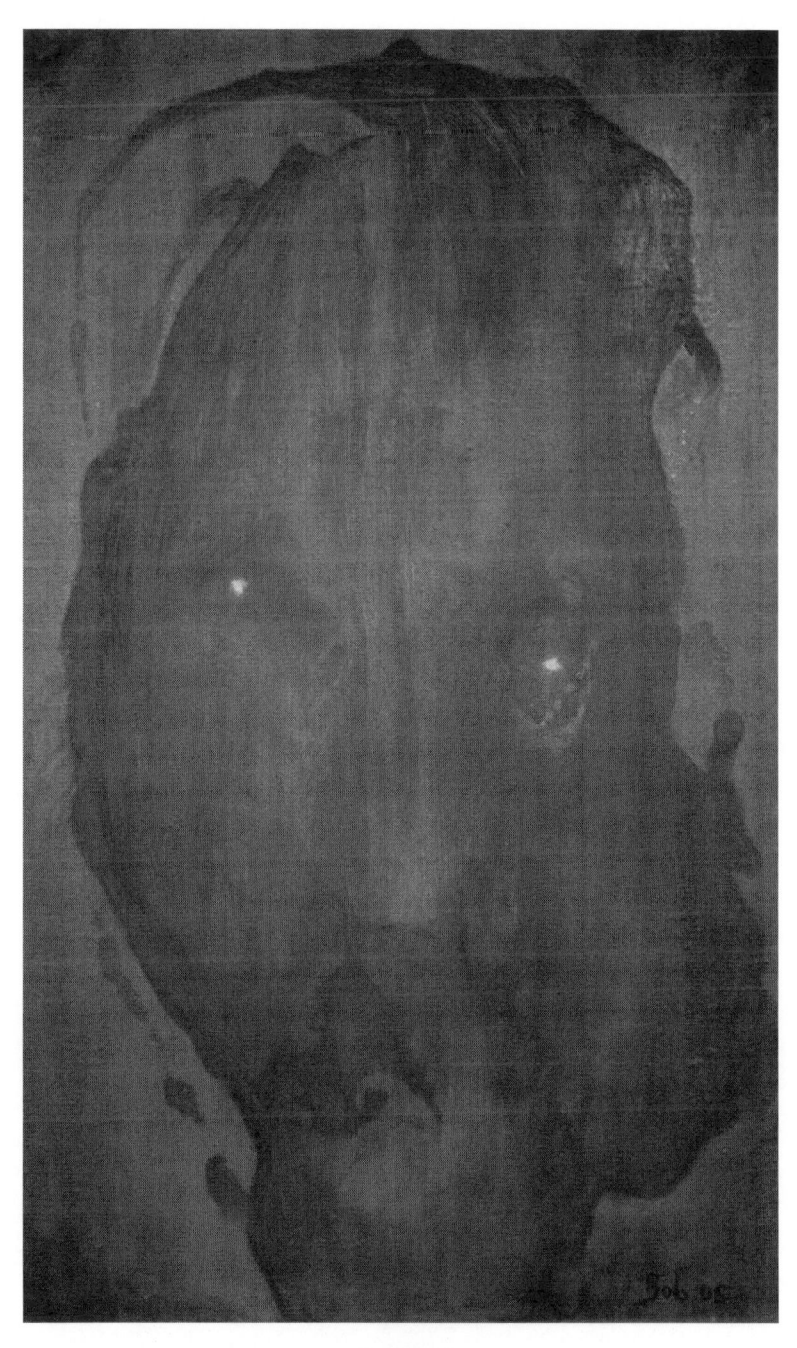

17

Selected by the minions
Old man scribbles
on a nebulous breakfast.

Sternum crotch and brain,
rejuvenation slows down
for a second
beneath his wrinkled skin.

There are seeds in the following,
in the aftermath and its future.
There are fissures on the run.

Cellular biomass entropy rolls.
Something is on the way.
He can smell
Ocean's breath on the sand.

Semantics is a matter of survival
amongst the non-important

the meaning of fish
in a sea of shiny swords
forged in malevolence.

Laminated days of dark memory,
lacquered by see-through winter's hush
in halls of what we can see,
Old man unlocks his hands
before the meeting with darkness.

It is all in the eye of the I.
Old man interprets the world
with a thermometer gone elevator.

Old man is no more.

"The Children, 2005"

ALSO AVAILABLE FROM ALIEN BUDDHA PRESS

Mar-a-Lago Teetotaler by Maxwell Ryder

The Art of Changing Nothing to Punk Gigs by Sudeep Adhikari

Acclimated Recollections by Felino Soriano

Prayer for the Outsider by Kenneth Trimble

Vegas Poems by Ryan Quinn Flanagan

Frenetic/No Contest by Dustin Pickering

Winds of Time by JoyAnne O'Donnell

Alien Buddha Cums to Jesus by Jay Miner and Jeff Flipski

The Headpoke And Firewedding by Paul Brookes

Dimensional High by Ammi Romero
Poison in Paradise by Scott Thomas Outlar

Meditations by Jonel Abellanosa

LOCOmotion of Life by Adam Levon Brown

My Name is Giorna Alzavola by Giorna Alzavola

Screamo Lullabies by Robert J.W

Surfing the Appalachian Vortex by Mark Hartenbach

Irritable Brain Syndrome by Willie Smith

About Consciousness by Heath Brougher

Heroin by Catfish McDaris

36 Haikus and a Horror Story by Red Focks

Vanilla, Lemon, Blood by Ron Androla

Icarus Rising by Don Beukes
Flakka Flakka by Ryan Quinn Flanagan

Our Little Hope by Bree

The Yellow Dot of a Daisy by Holly Day

Code 3 by Matt Borczon

A Taint of Pity by Ken Allan Dronsfield

Wire My Scars Electric by Zachary Dilks

Immaculate Days by Rus Khomutoff

Psalms of a Romantic Poet by Gideon Cecil

The Bleeding-Heart Poet by Ahmad Al-khatat

Mental by Warren Goff

Thread by Billy Antonio

Void Beneath the Skin by Mike Zone

An Occasional Death by Bud Ogden

Bartholomew: The Rapture by Ammi Romero

The Past is Calling by Thasia Anne

Witness Protection Program by Mark Hartenbach and Red Focks

Printed in Great Britain
by Amazon